CAREERS IN

ANTHROPOLOGY

ARCHAEOLOGY

AN ANCIENT INDIC LANGUAGE KNOWN as Sanskrit was "discovered" in the late 18th century by the British civil servant and intellectual, Sir William Jones. This discovery set the stage for intensive work in comparative historical linguistics that has continued ever since. In 2014, archaeologists in Egypt discovered the remains of a previously unknown pharaoh who reigned more than 3,600 years ago. What do linguistics and archaeology have in common? They are both scientific endeavors, pursued under the umbrella of anthropology.

Anthropology is the scientific study and analysis of human beings and humanity, including all the world's cultures, ethnicities, customs, artifacts, knowledge, habits, history, and languages. It emerged as a distinct academic discipline in England and America in the late 19th century and continues to expand its scope of study.

Anthropology is composed of four closely related fields.

Physical Anthropology

The first is physical (biological) anthropology, which studies the human being as a living organism. Population genetics and primatology are common areas of focus here.

Cultural Anthropology

The second, and largest specialty, is cultural anthropology. This involves studying specific populations up close and personal over long periods of time to learn more about their social and cultural patterns.

Linguistic Anthropology

The third field is linguistic anthropology, which focuses on language, from its origins, to how it affects complex social interactions in a modern, globally connected world.

Archaeology

The fourth field is archaeology, perhaps the most famous of the anthropological disciplines. Archaeologists can be found in the field, anywhere in the world, digging for artifacts, old bones, and other clues to how people lived in past cultures.

1

This is a great time to become an anthropologist. It has always been intellectually exciting. Today, more than ever, a degree in anthropology opens doors to a variety of career paths. Anthropologists have traditionally worked within the confines of academia, teaching and conducting research. This is no longer true. Anthropology graduates today are well-prepared for excellent jobs that require critical thinking skills in the realms of business, research, advocacy, and public service. Their training is uniquely well suited to the 21st century. The economy is increasingly international and, in turn, workforces and markets are more diverse. Anthropology is the primary discipline that helps people understand how communities and organizations work, even when they are separated by oceans and continents.

Anthropology offers many opportunities with good earnings, in both the public and private sectors. Anthropologists working for non-governmental organizations, such as international health organizations and development banks, help to design and implement a wide variety of programs worldwide. Many businesses look specifically for anthropologists, recognizing the value of their perspective on a corporate team as they struggle to understand consumer preference patterns not readily apparent through simple statistical or survey methods.

Agencies at all levels of government employ anthropologists to identify and protect cultural resources. Even local police departments need these professionals. Forensic anthropologists, in careers glamorized by Hollywood and popular novels, are called upon to help identify mysterious or unknown remains.

WHAT YOU CAN DO NOW

ARE YOU CONSIDERING A CAREER IN anthropology? Maybe you read about the many projects anthropologists are engaged in all over the world and think, I want to do that! If you are a high school student and have heard about anthropology, you are ahead of most people who eventually enter this profession. Many anthropologists are not even exposed to the subject until college. That means you already have a head start on preparing for your career.

Your high school curriculum should provide a strong foundation in history and other social sciences. You will also need courses in math (statistics is especially useful), physical sciences like biology and chemistry, as well as English and a foreign language. Also include any classes that would improve your computer skills, writing skills, and critical thinking.

Join as many associations as you can. The most influential is the American Anthropological Association (AAA). However, there are many others that are centered on particular topics, such as the Society for Medical Anthropology and the Society for Linguistic Anthropology. Every association offers information, scholarships, and programs for students. Some, like the Student Conservation Association, are dedicated to helping students.

Look for opportunities to volunteer, research, and study anthropology. There are tons of them available to high school students on up. The Anthropology Outreach Program at the Smithsonian Institution is a good place to start. Their internships offer student-mentor arrangements and other unique experiences for students, both in high school and college. The National Park Service has literally thousands of opportunities, offered in partnership with several national organizations. Internships of all kinds are offered, some outside in the field and some inside doing research, inventory and monitoring, interpretation, and education projects. Every August, the Park Service also conducts a career workshop in Washington DC. You can contact the park that interests you or go directly to the National Park Service website to investigate all of the opportunities nationwide.

Consider attending a field school. The best known is Crow Canyon Archaeological Center, in southwesern Colorado. It offers a three-week program for high school students to learn about the science of archaeology by researching the ancestral Pueblo Indians who inhabited the region hundreds of year ago. It takes place in the center of the richest archaeological region in the United States.

Passport in Time (PIT) is another field school of sorts. It is a volunteer archaeology and historic preservation program run by the USDA Forest Service. PIT volunteers work side by side with professional Forest Service archaeologists and historians on national forest sites throughout the US. The activities are amazingly diverse, from archaeological survey and excavation, to the analysis and curating of artifacts. Other activities include rock art restoration, surveys, archival research, restoration of historic structures, and gathering oral histories.

HISTORY OF THE PROFESSION

ANTHROPOLOGY IS THE STUDY OF THE entire history of humanity. The starting point is about 200,000 years ago when modern humans first evolved in Africa. Anthropologists have learned that humans started venturing beyond the boundaries of Africa when they crossed the Sinai Peninsula about 50,000 years ago. This fact was determined by dating human bones found in Israel. The trail did not stop there, of course. Humans quickly (relatively speaking) spread to several continents. Human fossils dating to 46,000 years ago have been found in Europe, Asia, and Australia. It was about 14,000 years ago that humans reached North America by crossing the Bering strait over a land con-

3

nection which is thought to have linked what is now Russia and Alaska, eventually arriving in what is now New Mexico.

In the tens of thousands of years of dispersal throughout the world, humanity has developed thousands of distinct cultures, languages, traditions, and tools. The goal of anthropology is to study all the differences and similarities between all the many societies and communities.

Considering the scope of anthropology and the immense time-span involved, one would think this is a well-established and mature profession. After all, the word "anthropology" was first added to the English language about 1600. However, it is one of the newest of the major scientific disciplines, though its development was long in the making with origins that can be traced back several centuries.

The origins of modern anthropology are rooted in the Age of Enlightenment of the 18th and early 19th centuries in Europe and North America. Also known as the Age of Reason, this period was marked by a cultural movement of intellectuals that emphasized reason and individualism rather than tradition. Its goal was to reform society by challenging superstition and religion, and advancing knowledge through scientific methods. This was done by the amateur anthropologists of the time who attempted to objectively record and understand variations in human cultures.

The early anthropologists were primarily motivated by curiosity. They simply wanted to know more about strange peoples and customs in far off parts of the world. They were not professional anthropologists, by any definition. Indeed, most were naturalists, medical doctors, Christian clerics, or educated explorers. They sought to answer basic questions that had never been asked before, such as whether cultural differences were genetic in origin, and whether there was a relationship between the size of the human body (specifically, the head) and intelligence.

It was not until the late 19th century that anthropology began to gain recognition as a distinct academic discipline in American and Western European universities. Today, of course, it is an international science, with anthropologists practicing their profession in most nations of the world.

Since its early development, anthropology has splintered into numerous highly focused specialties, such as archaeoastronomy, urban linguistics, and paleoanthropology. Each discipline, no matter how narrowly defined or obscure has developed its own unique set of scientific techniques to aid investigation.

While anthropology is endlessly fascinating to many, it faced problems for over a century from lack of public interest, to criticism from those who believed only the "hard" sciences have value. This trend is finally turning around, however, as the global economy is being influenced by the diffusion of people, technology, commodities, and ideas around the world.

WHERE THE JOBS ARE

ANTHROPOLOGISTS SEEM TO BE everywhere today, not just in a stuffy classroom or in exotic locales. You can find them studying the effects of poverty on urban crime in Detroit, studying DNA sequences in a sophisticated laboratory in Switzerland, immersing themselves in remote villages of the Amazonian rain forest, working in the aftermath of disasters like Hurricane Katrina and 9/11, or uncovering a 55-million-year-old primate on the coast of Mississippi.

Anthropology is a small profession. There are only about 7,500 of them in the US. Yet they make their presence known throughout the world, working in practically every environment and setting imaginable. Anthropologists work in deserts, cities, schools, even in underwater archaeological sites. Their employers range from small consulting firms to huge corporations like Intel and GM.

The largest employers of anthropologists, accounting for about half of the jobs are:

- Research and development in the social sciences and humanities
- Federal government
- Management, scientific, and technical consulting services

The other half of all jobs are not in categories, because the professional skills and knowledge are so commonly applied to a multitude of situations. In fact, you would be surprised at the different kinds of places anthropologists are finding work. The list of employers grows longer every day: research organizations, colleges and universities, museums, consulting firms, health and human services, community organizations, the media, private corporations, and all levels of government.

Anthropologists working in the public sector at state and local levels are employed by historical societies, community arts organizations, human services agencies, museums, state highway departments, and city health departments. Employment at the federal level comes from every agency you can name, from the US Forest Service to the USDA.

Anthropologists working in the private sector are often employed by corporations or businesses involved in domestic operations as well as international trade. Some work as research analysts in product development, market research, and advertising departments. Others work in human resources departments, helping global businesses with international employee relations and human resource management issues. Still others work in the field of technology development and technology transfer, helping to identify acceptance patterns of new technology, both in the US and abroad. There is also a

5

surprising number of anthropologists working in various departments in hospitals and at large university-affiliated medical centers. Their jobs typically involve research, teaching, and sometimes administrative duties. There are plenty of more unusual, yet important jobs, such as providing ethics consultations to physicians and families.

Not all anthropologists work as full-time employees. Some are self-employed independent consultants working on contract for agencies such as the Centers for Disease Control, UNESCO, the World Health Organization, and the World Bank.

Work Environment and Conditions As the work of anthropologists varies widely, so does the environment. An anthropologist might work in an office, a laboratory, or a lecture hall. Many anthropologists also work in the field. That can be a very stimulating environment! Fieldwork can take place anywhere in the United States or in the most remote foreign country. It often involves learning foreign languages, living in areas with few modern comforts, and seeing cultural conditions that most people would never imagine.

Anthropologists who work in government, in research and for consulting firms, museums, and businesses, typically stay close to home and work full time during normal business hours. Fieldwork is quite different. When doing fieldwork, anthropologists often travel for extended periods. Domestic field assignments typically last a month or two, but field assignments to remote areas or international locations can last much longer. Field workers must be able to adapt to changing environments and quickly integrate into new social circles. While the work is exciting, it can also be arduous. It often involves rugged living conditions and strenuous physical exertion. There is no set schedule – the hours can be long, including evenings, weekends, and holidays.

THE WORK YOU WILL DO

ANTHROPOLOGISTS ARE SCIENTISTS who study humanity, past and present. They explore what it means to be human by studying a range of cultural and social relations, human biology and evolution, languages, music and art, architecture, and the origins of human habitation. To understand the full scope and complexity of the human condition across the millennia of human history, anthropologists draw and build upon knowledge from the social and biological sciences, as well as the humanities and physical sciences. They use this knowledge to examine and compare the cultures, languages, archeological remains, and physical characteristics of people in all corners of the world.

Anthropologists are intensely curious. They seek to answer fascinating, and sometimes unanswerable questions, through the careful observation of humans and their behavior. What does it mean to be human? Why do people behave this way or that? How and why has their behavior changed over time? How could people from distant parts of the world, separated by oceans, be the same? What are the historical and environmental pressures that helped shape the experience of a specific group of people? What universal qualities are shared by all of human life?

It may seem that anthropologists are pure intellectuals, without any goal or purpose. On the contrary, the central concern of most anthropologists today is how to apply their research findings to the solution of human problems. Some of the issues they address are of major importance to everyone, such as overpopulation, warfare, poverty, and the effects of natural disasters. Sometimes the concerns are more localized or important only to governments or corporations who want to understand cultural differences in order to increase commerce in the global marketplace or improve living conditions around the world.

Anthropology is generally considered one of the social sciences, grouped together with psychology and sociology. However, it draws equally from the physical and life sciences. There are anthropologists who focus on non-physical features such as language – its role among humans, how it changes, and how differences affect relationships between cultures.

There are also anthropologists who study the human being as a living organism. Population genetics and primatology are common interests to physical anthropologists. For example, they might want to understand how humans have adapted to particular environments, both short term and long term. In this case, they might conduct physical research on the maternal physiological response to pregnancy in various climates, and the effects of the environment on both maternal and fetal well-being.

Although the type of work an anthropologist does can vary greatly depending on the particular employment and area of specialization, anthropologists do some or all of the following:

- Plan research projects and test hypotheses
- Develop data collection methods for a particular specialty or project
- Conduct interviews and surveys among specific demographic groups
- Record and manage information based on observations made in the field
- Collect and analyze data from documents and laboratory samples
- Prepare reports and present research findings

- Advise organizations on the cultural impact of policies, programs, and products
- Examine and compare the customs, values, and social patterns of different cultures

Anthropologists often use sophisticated tools and technologies in their work. The equipment used varies by task and specialty, but it typically includes excavating tools, laboratory equipment, statistical and database software, geophysical tools and equipment, and geographic information systems.

Anthropologists often specialize in one or more geographic areas of the world, such as West Africa, Latin America, the British Isles, Eastern Europe, North America, or Oceania. They may narrow their focus to particular populations in a locale or region. For example, one anthropologist might study the marriage rituals among Scots-Irish Americans in a suburban North Carolina community. Another might focus attention further away and research the use of economic cooperatives by the Pyrenees Basques and how they have been forced to modify their traditions to conform to the controlling Spanish and French legal structures. Still another might be fascinated by the aesthetic and linguistic aspects of Trinidadian calypso and "road songs."

Anthropology is a huge subject area that can be divided into many specific types of applied research. In general, however, American anthropologists have traditionally been trained in one of four broad fields: cultural anthropology, physical anthropology, archaeology, and linguistics. Each of the four utilizes distinctive skills, such as applying theories, employing research methodologies, formulating and testing hypotheses, and developing extensive sets of data. Addressing complex questions such as human origins, the past and present spread and treatment of infectious disease, or the positive and negative effects of globalization, requires synthesizing information from all four subfields. Therefore, while anthropologists often do highly specialized work, they are all highly trained generalists with a broad educational foundation in the four core areas of the science.

Cultural Anthropology

The most well-known branch of anthropology is probably cultural anthropology, also known as sociocultural anthropology. It involves the study of customs, cultures, and social lives of groups of people. Cultural anthropologists investigate social practices and processes in settings that range from remote, non-industrialized villages, to contemporary urban centers. They not only examine ancient or past cultures, but also modern societies.

8

The most famous anthropologist of all time was Margaret Mead, an American cultural anthropologist of the 20th century. Like Mead, many cultural anthropologists often spend time living in the societies they study, while they collect information through observations, interviews, and surveys. The focus is generally on how human beings interact with each other, ways they organize and govern themselves, behavior patterns and customs, and how they create meaning for their lives. Specific topics of concern include issues such as health, work, ecology and environment, education, technology, agriculture and development, and social change.

A hallmark of cultural anthropology is its concern with similarities and differences, both within and among societies, and its attention to race, sexuality, class, gender, and nationality. This area of anthropological research is distinguished by its emphasis on participant observation by gaining first-hand knowledge through close contact for extended periods of time. By placing oneself within the research context, the anthropologist is able to get a more accurate sense of how the subject population grapples with practical problems of everyday life – not to mention more esoteric issues of knowledge, truth, power, and justice.

Archaeology The best known anthropologists are the archaeologists. The focus of these professionals rests in the past. They study what remains of people who lived long ago, to piece together culture, history, and technologies, from the deepest prehistory to the recent past. They study and analyze material evidence, ranging from human remains, to artifacts, cave paintings, and ruins of ancient structures. Sometimes the evidence is obscure, marked only by subtle indications of past environments and landscapes. Other times there are hard physical objects, such as stone tools, mummified human remains, or pottery that can be scientifically tested for age and origin. Together, all the material evidence is examined within a prescribed theoretical context to answer questions about the history, customs, ideologies, social groupings, and living habits of people in earlier eras.

Archeologists also manage and protect archeological sites, commonly known as "digs." While this type of work looks exciting in the movies, it is anything but glamorous. In fact, during the excavation, everyday life can be quite tough. Archaeologists rise with the sun and start digging in the trenches, hoping to reveal more traces of the past that have not yet been unearthed at the site.

There is more to excavating than digging for artifacts. Overall, it is a carefully planned destruction of a site because once the site is dug, it no longer exists. Therefore, one of the most important tasks is to meticulously record as many details as possible, preserving not only the artifacts but many, many other types of information. Through the use of scientific methods, including some rather sophisticated technologies, a site can be reexamined forever through the notes, maps, samples, drawings, photographs, videos, and other data collected during the excavation.

Historical archaeologists focus on recovery and preservation of evidence and artifacts from past human cultures. Some work in national parks or at historical sites, providing site protection and educating the public. Others assess building sites to ensure that construction plans comply with federal regulations on site preservation. Archeologists often specialize in a particular geographic area or period, or type of objects studied, such as animal remains or underwater sites.

Archaeologists typically work in teams that include a variety of specialists. There may be team members who work only with domesticated plant remains, while others are expert in identifying manmade artifacts produced or imported into a particular area.

Physical Anthropology Physical anthropologists, also known as biological anthropologists, research the evolution of the human species. They look for early evidence of human life, analyze genetics, study primates, and examine the biological variations in humans. They analyze how culture and biology influence each other.

These anthropologists are especially interested in the origins of humans, evolution, and variations within populations. There are always more questions than answers that arise from research. How have humans adapted to diverse environments? How did biological processes cause disease and early death? How does culture affect growth, development, and behavior? Research can venture off into many directions. Some physical anthropologists study other primates (primatology) or fossil records (paleoanthropology). Some study prehistoric people (bioarchaeology) by examining human remains found at archeological sites. In this way, they can identify factors such as nutrition and disease that might have affected the populations. Still others rely on biology alone (health, hormones, growth and development) to determine the genetics of past and living populations. These professionals may work as forensic anthropologists in medical or legal settings, identifying and analyzing skeletal remains and genetic material.

Linguistic Anthropology Linguistic anthropologists are concerned with how humans communicate and how language shapes social life. Research is generally focused on the structure and development of languages, and the differences among languages. These anthropologists examine the role of language in different cultures, how those cultures affect language, and how language affects an individual's experiences. Their investigations include both verbal and nonverbal communication. Most linguistic anthropologists study non-European languages, which they learn directly from native speakers. Linguistic anthropology shares with anthropology in general, a desire to understand power, inequality, and social change, particularly as these are constructed and represented through language and discussion.

Like all anthropology fields, linguistic anthropology is a comparative study. In this case, it compares the many ways in which language reflects and influences social life in different populations. For example, it may be used to explore how language is used to define patterns of communication within a population, and how it forms categories of social identity and group membership. It can examine how language has been historically used to organize large-scale cultural beliefs, religions, and ideologies in different regions.

In contemporary times, linguistic anthropologists are often called upon to compare the non-Western forms of exchange and value to the study of capitalism, from stock markets to the anti-globalization movement. They may investigate how language is used to legitimize, authorize, and contest such issues as nation-building, non-governmental activism, human rights, and the global "war on terror."

STORIES OF WORKING ANTHROPOLOGISTS

I Am an Archaeologist "Archaeology is a great career, but it is not as glamorous as the movies would have you believe. In fact, it is very hard work. In the field, it involves extensive physical labor in all kinds of weather. If you don't like getting your hands dirty, this is not the career for you. After all, it's called a 'dig' because you are digging in the dirt. You have to be fit and healthy and willing to forego fashion for sensible shoes and grubby clothes. The job also imposes a multitude of inconveniences. Archaeological sites are rarely located near shops, restaurants, or even comfortable hotels. You have to be ready to rough it for a few weeks at a time, sleeping on the ground, cooking on a camp stove, going for days without a shower, and those grubby clothes – they're going to stay grubby.

Of course, I don't dig all the time. I have many responsibilities. When I'm off the dig, I'm writing about it. One of the most important jobs of an archaeologist is reporting on the results of an excavation. An excavation site is constantly changing, and disappearing as it goes. If it is not properly recorded, the information about the site is lost forever. For that reason, I tell students who are interested in archaeology to make sure their writing skills are well-honed.

Despite all the dirt, sweat, and paperwork, I have enjoyed every single day on the job. It is great fun, and yet I take my responsibilities very seriously. I must always be careful with what I dig up. The remains of the past must always be available to others for future study."

I Am a Cultural Anthropologist "When I tell people I am an anthropologist, they stare blankly at me and ask, 'But what do you actually do?' It's not an easy question to answer because my activities are so diverse.

I spend part of my life in the field. 'The field' can be anywhere – a gold mine in Ghana, a community center in Harlem, or a village in Haiti. My goal in the field is to collect data. That means immersing myself in the environment, closely interacting with the people there. I live as they do, attend their events, discuss matters of importance to them, read the same books as they do, participate in daily routines of shopping and cooking, and join in celebrations and traditions.

When I am not in the field, I am usually at my desk writing about what I've learned. This is sometimes hard after being very socially active in the field. It sometimes takes a few days to settle into the quieter routine of reading, thinking, and writing. Describing and analyzing my fieldwork experiences are a slow and often painstaking process. It often takes weeks and sometimes months and the result can look more like a book than a 'report,' though my goal is far less ambitious. My intent is to write in simple terms what I've learned from my observations and hope my contributions shape the knowledge of future anthropologists."

PERSONAL QUALIFICATIONS

EMPLOYERS LOOK FOR PERSONAL characteristics such as intelligence, friendliness, good work habits, and how well you fit into a group. These traits tend to come out in interviews. There are many other valuable skills that cannot be demonstrated with a résumé or in conversation, yet they are necessary in order to succeed in this profession.

Knack for Research

All anthropologists have knowledge of scientific methods and data collection techniques used in research. They know how to interview individuals, comb through artifacts and references, conduct laboratory experiments, and draw logical conclusions from observations. The most successful anthropologists also have a special talent for identifying the kind of research projects that attract attention and support from universities, the federal government, and other organizations willing to commit funding dollars.

An aptitude for research also means having the patience to dig out answers to difficult questions. It can take a long time to learn new things about other cultures.

Critical Thinking Skills

Anthropologists must be able to combine pieces of information to try to solve problems and to answer research questions. To do this well, an anthropologist needs analytical intelligence, skill at mathematics (statistics in particular), and an open mind. The answers do not usually come easily. It takes intelligence to find the best ways to overcome the obstacles that inevitably arise during the course of a project. The ability to design experiments or data collecting projects, make accurate observations, and correctly analyze findings are also vital to the process.

Intellectual Curiosity

The power of curiosity cannot be underestimated. Successful anthropologists have an enduring curiosity to wade through myriad details in search of interesting revelations, and to delve into cultures and time periods very different from their own.

Good Communications Skills

Strong writing skills are needed for writing reports that detail research findings. Ideally, the reports will reach a relatively wide audience. It is not uncommon to have research findings published in both scholarly journals and public interest publications, so the language must be understood by professional colleagues and laymen alike. Being able to present an argument based on findings is also key. Anthropologists are typically fluent in several languages, which is necessary when traveling to other countries to conduct research. Sometimes, they have to talk to people who do not understand any of the known languages. In those cases, the anthropologist must be able to use body language to communicate.

Thirst for Knowledge

Like all scientific disciplines, the field of anthropology is always growing and evolving. In order to stay on the forefront of the field, successful anthropologists constantly read scientific journals, attend conferences, and discuss findings with colleagues.

ATTRACTIVE FEATURES

ANTHROPOLOGISTS CAN CHOOSE from a variety of work settings. Many anthropologists choose to work as college and university professors, where they move from the lecture hall, to the research laboratory, to a quiet office to write for publication. It is a stimulating atmosphere that fosters intellectual discourse and a sense of community with like-minded individuals.

Anthropologists are no longer limited to academia. Today they work for all kinds of businesses, large and small, as well as a wide range of government agencies. Many jobs offer the opportunity for travel – around the country and around the world.

Although anthropology is a relatively small profession, the range of opportunities is one of the leading benefits of this field. Anthropology has splintered into countless highly focused fields. Today's anthropologists can work in a range of specialties under the umbrellas of archaeology, linguistics, cultures, or human physical development. The nature of anthropological work and the numerous specialties make anthropology an intellectually stimulating career.

Nobody goes into anthropology to become wealthy. However, most anthropologists can expect to earn a comfortable living. Anthropologists earn an average of about $60,000 per year, but that is just an average. Top earners who have published successful books reportedly can earn up to $135,000.

The job outlook is good. Anthropology is a fairly stable field for those with the requisite education and field experience. For aspiring anthropologists, the good news is that there will be higher-than-average growth in employment for anthropologists for the foreseeable future. Job prospects will be competitive, especially for those who do not possess graduate degrees.

UNATTRACTIVE ASPECTS

ALTHOUGH IT IS POSSIBLE TO EARN A good living, starting pay for beginning anthropologists is low. This is especially true for those who only hold bachelor's degrees. To earn top pay, it is necessary to obtain at least a master's degree, and a doctorate is recommended. That is a heavy investment for the financial return when compared to some other professions.

While anthropologists often enjoy field work and the opportunities to see the world, the travel can get exhausting. You may spend months in a remote location with little communication access to home. Some archeologists are away from home as long as 280 days a year! That can be very hard on relationships and family life. Making friends outside the profession can be difficult. While working in the field, the hours are long and hard. There are always research deadlines to meet and often there is limited funding for projects. As a result, fieldwork can be stressful and exhausting.

Anthropology can be physically challenging. It is not just about book learning and talking with people. Sometimes you have to get your hands dirty in site excavations. Some dig sites are located in hot, treacherous climates, and in hard to access locations.

Finding and landing the perfect job is not easy. Although the job outlook is very good and there are more subspecialties being created, it is still a small field. The number of graduates often outpaces the available job openings.

EDUCATION AND TRAINING

THE EDUCATION REQUIREMENTS CAN be demanding for any scientific field, and anthropology is no exception. A bachelor's degree will not count for much on an application to become an anthropologist, but a four-year college degree is certainly the starting point. Bachelor's degree holders may find jobs as laboratory technicians, research assistants, fieldworkers, or writers. They may also find employment in one of the many related fields, or in the private sector working for a corporation or business as a consultant, analyst, or market researcher.

When planning courses, keep in mind that anthropology draws on a wide educational foundation. Courses in both social and physical sciences as well as the humanities will be very useful. So are communications skills, foreign languages, computer skills, and the arts. You most likely will not know what specific area of anthropology you will end up focusing on until after completing the core curriculum, but you should prepare as best you can. A faculty advisor in the anthropology department can help you design a course of study that best suits your interests.

Anthropology is a field where grades matter. Some employers may not need to see your academic transcript, but many others will want to. Grades have other consequences. They indicate that you have the kind of positive work habits needed in the field. They also raise your general visibility with professors, who will be your first networking contacts. Teachers are always more willing to write strong letters of recommendation, something which every potential employer will want to see, for students who work hard and excel.

Undergraduate Degrees
Bachelor's degrees in anthropology will usually require four years. The exact course requirements will vary by university, but in addition to meeting core requirements, the degree will typically require classes in demographic anthropology, economic anthropology, the origins of language, food and culture, human origins, and disease in antiquity.

Students who are not planning on continuing their education past college should consider doing a double major. This will help broaden their employment opportunities. Study in fields such as business, nursing, public health, marketing, international trade, and linguistics are particularly useful in the job market.

Master's Degree
More than half of all anthropologists hold at least a master's degree. With this degree, graduates can teach at community or junior colleges, qualify for positions as applied anthropologists, or continue their postgraduate education.

It normally takes two years to complete the requirements for a master's degree in anthropology. Each university will have different requirements and courses, but a typical program will require a field research project that lasts several months, fluency in at least one foreign language, and a thesis. Typical courses include anthropological research design, seminars in medical anthropology, sociocultural theory, physical anthropology, and applied anthropology.

16

Doctoral Degree

Almost half of all anthropologists have earned their doctoral degrees. Although a master's degree is enough for many positions, a PhD is often necessary for jobs that require leadership skills and advanced technical knowledge. In order to direct projects outside the United States, anthropologists and archeologists typically need a PhD to comply with the requirements of foreign governments.

Specific requirements vary by institution, but a typical program generally takes several years to complete. Some universities allow students to apply up to a third of the credits from their master's programs, assuming the courses are closely related.

Students should expect to take courses in their doctoral program in all major areas of anthropology including archaeology, linguistics, sociocultural anthropology, and biological anthropology. In addition, PhD candidates must pass an examination and defend their dissertations. PhD students typically spend between 12 and 36 months doing field research for their dissertation.

Field Experience In order to get a job, new anthropologists usually need hands-on experience in the field, plus training in a variety of research methods. Some candidates fulfill this requirement by conducting field research as part of their graduate program. Others do internships with museums, historical societies, or nonprofit organizations. They may work with objects at museums or travel abroad to assist with research projects. Some attend archeological field schools, where they receive practical training through actual archaeological digs. They learn basic important skills such as how to excavate historical and archeological sites, how to record findings, and how to interpret the data.

EARNINGS

SALARY LEVELS RANGE WIDELY FOR anthropologists. Several factors affect salary levels, including the employer, prior experience, level of education, and the geographic location of the job. At the upper end of the salary range, a small number of practicing anthropologists earn well in excess of $100,000 annually – as much as $135,000 for published professionals. A substantial portion of that comes through royalties from publications. The lowest 10 percent earn less than $35,000. The lower wage earners are typically part-time workers, or those with the least amount of experience.

Overall, anthropologists earn about $60,000 annually, on average.

The starting salary of an anthropology major with an undergraduate degree is only about $40,000, according to a National Association of Colleges and Employers salary survey. Starting salaries depend on the type of degree an anthropologist has. A graduate with a bachelor's degree, for example, will start out at a lower salary level than a candidate with a master's or doctoral degree. Salaries rise significantly with more education, primarily because master's and doctoral degrees qualify anthropologists for high-paying positions in academia, federal government, and overseas research.

Earnings also vary considerably by location. The highest paid anthropologists can be found in Washington DC, most likely because that is where the majority of federal jobs are. Anthropologists in the District of Columbia are paid an average annual salary of about $95,000. Those in Massachusetts and Hawaii earn the next highest salaries of $75,000 and $70,000, respectively. Anthropologists would be closer to the industry average in California, Texas, and Pennsylvania. The average annual salaries in these three states are around $65,000. Anthropologists working for the federal government earn the highest yearly salaries of any employment outside of academia. Top paying employers for anthropologists also include:

Museums and historical sites
$65,000

Local government agencies
$60,000

Management consulting firms
$60,000

State government
$55,000

Scientific and technical consulting services
$55,000

Research and development services
$50,000

Traditionally, there have been more anthropologists working for universities than any other employer. Although the field has grown far beyond the hallowed walls of academia, that basic fact has not changed. Anthropologists who earn master's or doctoral degrees often become college and university professors. They can earn income from teaching anthropology classes, pursuing their own research (funded by grants which they must obtain), and writing books and journal articles for publication. Becoming an anthropology professor at a university generally requires a PhD, while a master's degree may suffice for employment at a community college. Anthropologists at universities earn on average about $85,000, while those at two-year colleges average $80,000.

OPPORTUNITIES

THE JOB OUTLOOK FOR ANTHROPOLOGISTS is better than most occupations can expect. Employment is expected to grow almost 20 percent over the next decade. Because it is a small field, the fast growth will result in only about 1,500 new jobs during that time. Still, in general, there is a growing need for anthropologists to study human life, history, and culture, and to apply that knowledge to current issues.

Traditionally, most anthropologists have been found in the academic arena, conducting research and teaching. Today, a growing number of jobs are opening up on college campuses in departments other than anthropology. A number of academic anthropologists are now finding jobs in schools of medicine, epidemiology, public health, ethnic studies, cultural studies, community or area studies, linguistics, education, ecology, cognitive psychology, and neural science. Those involved in pure research are usually highly dependent on the availability of research funding. Therefore, federal budgetary decisions will continue to affect the rate of employment growth in research regardless of the specific subject matter.

In general, the strongest job growth will be in the private sector. As global commerce continues to grow, corporations will increasingly use anthropological research to gain a better understanding of consumer demand within specific cultures or social groups. Anthropologists will also be called upon to analyze markets, both foreign and domestic, to gain insight into the needs and desires of new customers or demographic groups.

Perhaps the best job prospects will be in cultural resource management (CRM) firms. Cultural resource managers are typically in charge of museums, galleries, and theaters that focus on culture specific to the local region or ethnic group. Virtually all large natural history museums and some art museums have anthropologists on staff conducting research and helping to develop exhibits. One of the growth fields has been planning and directing educational activities for the public.

Some anthropologists will also find opportunities as tour guides. Cultural tourism has become a significant sector of the tourism industry. Candidates with experience in both qualitative and quantitative research methods who can communicate findings to a wide variety of audiences will be in great demand. However, due to the high interest in this type of work, the competition for jobs is fairly strong.

Anthropologists fill the range of career niches occupied by other social scientists in corporations, government, nonprofit corporations, and various trade and business settings. Many corporations look explicitly for anthropologists, recognizing the utility of their perspective on a corporate team. How-

19

ever, the majority of positions filled by anthropologists do not mention the word anthropologist in the job announcement. Instead, the job postings call for researchers, evaluators, and project managers. The unique training and perspective of anthropologists enable them to compete successfully for these jobs.

GETTING STARTED

THERE MAY BE NO COLLEGE MAJOR more fascinating than anthropology. It is great to be intrigued by your studies, but at some point you must go out and look for a job. There will be jobs available to you if you know where to look and how to go about getting one.

Start Looking

Review the variety of sources for information about job opportunities. It is not going to be as easy as looking for ads in your local newspaper for "anthropologist wanted." Typically, you will not see help wanted ads for pure anthropologist positions outside of a university setting. So where do you find job openings? Look to the organizations in your field. For example, positions are advertised in the American Anthropological Association's Anthropology Newsletter and on the AAA's job boards. Also check your college career center. This should be a key component in your job search. In addition to job postings, you will find valuable services such as career and employment counseling, employer and graduate school information, workshops on résumé writing, help with interviewing skills, and more.

Volunteer

Spending a few hours a week volunteering could be the best investment you will ever make in your career. Consider this: most of the other people in any volunteering situation are usually volunteers themselves, and they have contacts. If you make a point to get to know them through your volunteering, they might be impressed enough to connect you with people who have jobs available or even offer you a job that they have. Sometimes the volunteer organization itself will offer you a job, if you have shown how dedicated and thoughtful you are. Volunteering is not a quick way to employment. It might take a few months to yield results, so you might need to find alternative ways to support yourself in the meantime.

Intern

An internship can have a profound effect on your career. It can be a great way to get the kind of practical hands-on experience employers want to see on your résumé. This adds to your potential recommendations and puts you in a better position to get a full-time paying job. An internship can also give

20

you a chance to make contacts in your field. Sometimes an internship can even develop into a full-time job.

Network

The use of interpersonal networks is a traditional anthropological tool. In planning a career as a practicing anthropologist, you will need to cultivate networks with other practicing anthropologists. The fastest way to build a network of contacts who may help you find work later is to volunteer or intern, but there are other ways. You can join professional organizations and attend meetings and regional conferences. You can become involved in a mentoring program such as the NAPA Mentor Program (National Association of Student Anthropologists). In this program students are paired with practicing anthropologists. Their interaction may take many forms, including discussions and help with job search or career issues.

Be Flexible

Do not get stuck on an idea of exactly where you want to work or how you are willing to apply your knowledge and skills. If you want to work as a full-time anthropologist, it is important to be willing to relocate. You may want to stay close to home, but other regions of the country may be better locations for your particular skills. You should also consider employment overseas, which is a continually expanding job market.

Keep in mind that there are many different kinds of jobs for anthropology graduates. Your training and skills could qualify you for work in intercultural training, refugee services, policy science, curating, city planning, housing administration, social work, survey research, or market analysis, just to name a few possibilities. You must be prepared to present your case. Since many employers are not sure what anthropologists are or what they have been trained to do, you should be ready to describe specific details about your abilities that would be beneficial to the position or organization.

ASSOCIATIONS

- **American Anthropological Association**
  http://www.aaanet.org

- **Society for Applied Anthropology**
  http://www.sfaa.net

- **Archaeological Institute of America**
  http://www.archaeological.org

- **American Association of Physical Anthropologists**
  http://physanth.org

- **National Association for the Practice of Anthropology**
  http://practicinganthropology.org/

- **Society for American Archaeology**
  http://www.saa.org/

- **Society for Medical Anthropology**
  http://www.medanthro.net

- **Society for Linguistic Anthropology**
  http://linguisticanthropology.org

- **The Archaeological Convervancy**
  www.archaeologicalconservancy.org

- **Federation of Small Anthropology Programs**
  www.aaanet.org/sections/gad/fosap

- **Consortium of Practicing and Applied Anthropology Programs**
  http://www.copaa.info

- **The Student Conservation Association**
  http://www.thesca.org

- **National Association of Student Anthropologists**
  www.studentanthropologists.org

PERIODICALS

- **Archaeology Magazine**
  http://www.archaeology.org

- **Popular Archaeology**
  http://popular-archaeology.com

- **Dig**
  http://www.digonsite.com

- **Popular Anthropology Magazine**
  http://popanthro.org/ojs/index.php/popanthro

- **Scientific American**
  www.scientificamerican.com/topic.cfm?id=anthropology

- **Student Conservation Association**
  https://www.thesca.org

WEBSITES

- Anthropology at the Smithsonian Institution http://anthropology.si.edu/index.html

- University of Michigan, Department of Anthropology http://www.lsa.umich.edu

- Harvard University, Department of Anthropology http://anthropology.fas.harvard.edu

- University of California, Berkeley http://anthropology.berkeley.edu

- Day of Archaeology http://www.dayofarchaeology.com

- Smithsonian Institution, National Museum of Natural History, Academic Opportunities & Programs www.nmnh.si.edu/rtp/other_opps

- Crow Canyon Archaeological Center www.crowcanyon.org/Archaeology_Adventures/Summer_Camps.asp

- Passport In Time www.passportintime.com

- Rick Hick's Internships in Anthropology http://rhicks.iweb.bsu.edu/intern.htm